A HORRID FACTBO

HORRID HENRY'S
DINOSAURS

**Francesca Simon** spent her childhood on the beach in California, and then went to Yale and Oxford universities to study medieval history and literature. She now lives in London with her family. She has written over fifty books, and won the Children's Book of the Year in 2008 at the Galaxy British Book Awards for *Horrid Henry and the Abominable Snowman*.

**Tony Ross** is one of Britain's best-known illustrators, with many picture books to his name as well as line c

For a complete list of **Horrid Henry** titles
visit www.horridhenry.co.uk

Also by Francesca Simon

*Don't Cook Cinderella*
*Helping Hercules*

and for younger readers

*Don't Be Horrid, Henry*
Illustrated by Kevin McAleenan

*The Parent Swap Shop*
Illustrated by Pete Williamson

*Spider School*
Illustrated by Tony Ross

*The Topsy-Turvies*
Illustrated by Emily Bolam

# A HORRID FACTBOOK

# HORRID HENRY'S DINOSAURS

## Francesca Simon
### Illustrated by Tony Ross

Orion
Children's Books

First published in Great Britain in 2011
by Orion Children's Books
a division of the Orion Publishing Group Ltd
Orion House
5 Upper Saint Martin's Lane
London WC2H 9EA
An Hachette UK Company

1 3 5 7 9 10 8 6 4 2

Facts compiled by Sally Byford.

ISBN 978 1 4440 0447 2

A catalogue record for this book
is available from the British Library.

Printed in Great Britain by Clays Ltd, St Ives plc

# CONTENTS

# Dinosaur Hello

**Hello fellow dino fans!!!**

**Welcome to my fantastic new book about all things dinosaur! Wouldn't it be great to have your own Tyranosaurus rex, or Velociraptor, or Giganotosaurus available when pesky people like Moody Margaret dropped by? Or when annoying little brothers kept barging into your bedroom? Or when teachers tried to tell you off? Ha!**

Well, if a handy T-rex isn't around when you need one, this blood-curdling, bone crunching, flesh-creeping book will be the next best thing. Just wait til you discover how big a T-rex poo was, or how much it could eat in ONE mouthful . . . (Peter, Margaret, Steve, Bill, Miss Battle-Axe . . .)

Yeah!

Henry

# FIRST FACTS

# Mesozoic Period
## 'The Age of the Reptiles'

## Triassic
### 245–208 million years ago

The first dinosaurs appeared, like:

*Plateosaurus* (right)

*Procompsognathus*

*Saltopus*

## Jurassic
### 208–146 million years ago

Different types of dinosaurs spread across the world, like:

*Allosaurus*

*Apatosaurus*

*Compsognathus*

*Diplodocus*

*Stegosaurus*

*Brachiosaurus* (right)

## Cretaceous
### 146–65 million years ago

Even more different types of dinosaurs appeared, like:

*Tyrannosaurus rex*
*Triceratops* (below)
*Iguanodon*
*Ankylosaurus*
*Deinonychus*
*Dromaeosaurus*
*Velociraptor*

---

# Then all the dinosaurs died out.

The word 'dinosaur' means 'terrible lizard'.

A dinosaur is a type of reptile that stands upright, with its legs positioned directly under its body. Other reptiles, like crocodiles and lizards, have legs that sprawl out to the side.

Dinosaurs ruled the Earth for **160 million years**.

Human beings have only been around for about **4–5 million years**, so we've got a long way to go to beat the dinosaurs' record!

The time when the dinosaurs lived on Earth is called the **Mesozoic** period or 'The Age of the Reptiles'. It is divided into three shorter periods – **Triassic**, **Jurassic** and **Cretaceous**.

Different species of dinosaurs lived during each of these three periods. You might have seen a **Tyrannosaurus rex** bump into a **Stegosaurus** in a film, but it could never have happened in real life.

# FANTASTIC FOSSILS

We know lots of amazing facts about dinosaurs because of the fossil rocks discovered by scientists.

Scientists study **dinosaur fossils** and compare their findings with animals that are alive today. That's how we know what dinosaurs looked like.

Fossils aren't always bones – they can be footprints, eggs, skin and even droppings.

Just like the dinosaurs they discover, the scientists who study them also have a long name – **palaeontologists**.

By working out the age of fossil rocks, palaeontologists can tell when a dinosaur was alive.

People have been digging up dinosaur fossils for **thousands of years** without knowing what they were …

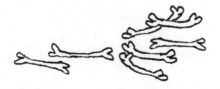

. . . In China about 2,000 years ago, people thought they'd discovered **dragon bones**, and in England in 1676 people believed they'd found a giant's thighbone.

But in fact they were all dinosaur bones!

The first time a scientist realised he'd found the bones of a new and exciting reptile was in England in 1822. He named it **Iguanodon**, meaning **'iguana tooth'**, because its teeth were the same shape as a modern iguana's – but a lot bigger. The name 'dinosaur' wasn't actually invented until nearly **20 years later**.

Dinosaurs have been found everywhere except **Antarctica**, where there's too much snow and ice.

America and Canada are the **best places** to dig for dinosaur fossils, especially in the desert – because there are only a few cactuses to get in the way.

Scientists don't often find a complete skeleton, but they can guess how **big** a dinosaur was from just **one bone**.

Fossil bones sometimes have marks where muscles were attached – this helps scientists to work out the shape of a dinosaur's body.

Did you know that over **650** different kinds of dinosaur have been discovered so far . . . ?

. . . And more than **ten** new dinosaurs are discovered every year!

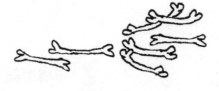

# PREHISTORIC
# SUPERSTARS

**Apatosaurus** – a huge, harmless plant-eater with a bulky body and a tiny brain.

**Brachiosaurus** – a massive monster with a very long neck that munched on leaves from the tallest trees.

**Stegosaurus** – a pin-headed, plant-eater with diamond-shaped plates on its back and tail.

**Triceratops** – a heavy three-horned dinosaur with a bony neck frill.

**Tyrannosaurus rex** – a terrifying flesh-eater, with a huge head, large, pointed teeth and two powerful legs. T-rex wasn't actually the biggest or the fiercest, but he's still everyone's favourite flesh-eater . . . at a distance!

**Velociraptor** – a fast and fierce meat-eater with one large and lethal curved claw on each foot.

# B-LIST
# BEASTS

**Allosaurus** – this meat-eater feasted on stegosaurs.

**Compsognathus** – a hen-sized carnivore with two long, thin legs.

**Deinonychus** – a fast and very fierce dinosaur that attacked its prey by slashing out with the long curved claws on its feet and biting off chunks of flesh with its razor-sharp teeth.

**Diplodocus** – a plant-eating dinosaur with a long, thin neck, a whip-like tail and nostrils on top of its head.

**Dromaeosaurus** – a small, fast-moving dinosaur with an especially sharp claw on each foot.

**Gallimimus** – a speedy bird-like dinosaur without any teeth.

**Giganotosaurus** – this enormous meat-eating dinosaur was even larger than the terrifying Tyrannosaurus rex, but it was discovered much later when T-rex was already the best-known and most popular dinosaur.

**Herrerasaurus** – a meat-eating dinosaur the size of a horse, with knife-shaped teeth for slicing up food.

**Iguanodon** – about the height of a double-decker bus, this dinosaur had small hooves on three fingers of each hand so it could walk just as well on two legs as it could on four.

**Microraptor** – a four-winged gliding dinosaur, covered in feathers.

**Oviraptor** – this small, speedy bird-like dinosaur liked to eat both meat and plants.

**Plateosaurus** – a plant-eater with small leaf-shaped teeth.

**Sauroposeidon** – a huge plant-eater with an even longer neck than Brachiosaurus.

**Spinosaurus** – a funny-looking flesh-eater with a sail on its back.

**Stegoceras** – a medium-sized plant-eater, with a thick skull.

**Styracosaurus** – a horned dinosaur with a spiny frill around its neck and a tall horn on its nose.

**Troodon** – a fast-moving flesh-eater, about the size of an adult human being.

**Utahraptor** – this speedy flesh-eater hunted in a pack.

# A-Z OF
# ALSO-RANS

**Acanthopolis** – a dinosaur with an armour of plates on its body and sharp spikes along the middle of its back.

**Anatosaurus** – this dinosaur had a broad snout like a duck's beak, and a layer of skin over its hands like a duck's webbed feet.

**Anchisaurus** – a small, lightly-built dinosaur with large clawed thumbs.

**Argentinosaurus** – a gigantic, but not very well-known, plant-eater.

**Coelurus** – a small, light dinosaur with a tiny skull the size of a human hand.

**Corythosaurus** – a large, plant-eating duck-billed dinosaur with a bony crest on its head that looked like a flattened helmet.

**Edmontosaurus** – a flat-headed dinosaur with a wide duck-like beak.

**Megalosaurus** – a fierce meat-eater with jagged teeth.

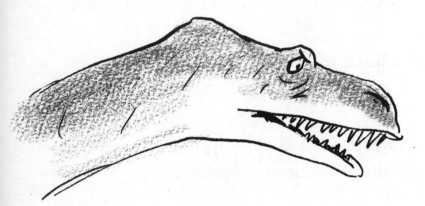

**Nodosaurus** – a heavy plant-eating dinosaur, with armoured plates on its body and tail.

**Pachycephalosaurus** – a plant-eating, dome-headed dinosaur.

**Parasaurolophus** – a duck-billed, long-crested plant-eater.

**Procompsognathus** – one of the earliest and tiniest meat-eaters, weighing only one kilogram, about the weight of a small melon.

**Riojasaurus** – one of the earliest and stupidest of the plant-eating dinosaurs.

**Saltopus** – this agile little lizard-eater is one of the oldest known dinosaurs.

**Saurolophus** – a duck-billed dinosaur with a spiked forehead.

**Seismosaurus** – a tiny-brained, plant-eating giant with a whip-like tail.

**Silvisaurus** – an armoured plant-eater.

**Stygimoloch** – a plant-eater with strange spikes and bumps on its skull.

**Torosaurus** – a long and large dinosaur with a huge horned skull.

# FEARSOME
# FAMILIES

When palaeontologists discover a new dinosaur, they have to fit it into the **dinosaur family tree.** This is a bit like your own family tree, with all your brothers, sisters, aunts, uncles and cousins, but a lot more complicated.

There are two main groups of dinosaurs – the **saurischians** and the **ornithischians**. Every dinosaur is a member of one of these two groups.

The difference between the two groups is the structure of their hip bones.

**Saurischians** have hip bones like lizards; **ornithischians** have hip bones like birds.

The **saurischians** included flesh-eaters (theropods) and plant-eaters (sauropods); all the **ornithischians** were plant-eaters.

# Henry's Easy-Peasy Dinosaur Family Tree

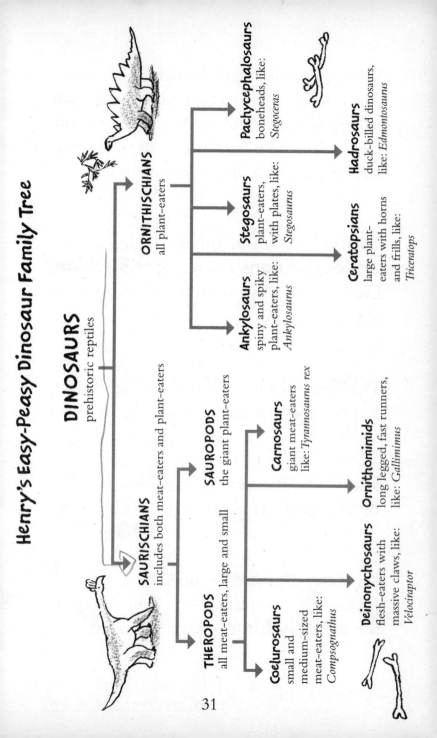

**DINOSAURS**
prehistoric reptiles

**SAURISCHIANS**
includes both meat-eaters and plant-eaters

**ORNITHISCHIANS**
all plant-eaters

**THEROPODS**
all meat-eaters, large and small

**SAUROPODS**
the giant plant-eaters

**Coelurosaurs**
small and
medium-sized
meat-eaters, like:
*Compsognathus*

**Deinonychosaurs**
flesh-eaters with
massive claws, like:
*Velociraptor*

**Carnosaurs**
giant meat-eaters
like: *Tyrannosaurus rex*

**Ornithominids**
long legged, fast runners,
like: *Gallimimus*

**Ankylosaurs**
spiny and spiky
plant-eaters, like:
*Ankylosaurus*

**Stegosaurs**
plant-eaters,
with plates, like:
*Stegosaurus*

**Pachycephalosaurs**
boneheads, like:
*Stegoceras*

**Ceratopsians**
large plant-
eaters with horns
and frills, like:
*Triceratops*

**Hadrosaurs**
duck-billed dinosaurs,
like: *Edmontosaurus*

31

# SUPER-SIZE DINOS

Giant plant-eaters like **Brachiosaurus** needed extra-strong tree-trunk legs and large padded feet to carry their huge bodies.

**Argentinosaurus** measured 35 metres long by nine metres wide – that's the size of a public swimming pool!

One shin-bone from an **Argentinosaurus** measured nearly two metres long – the height of a very tall man.

Even the smallest of the sauropods, like **Anchisaurus**, were as big as a car.

**Brachiosaurus** reached as high as six people standing on top of each other and could have looked over a three-storey house.

**Brachiosaurus** weighed up to 89 tonnes – the same as 12 elephants.

But the **Blue Whale** still beats the record for the heaviest animal at 150 tonnes – more than 21 elephants.

**Riojasaurus** could kill a smaller dinosaur with one swipe of its **massive tail**.

**Tyrannosaurus rex** was about 14 metres long and six metres high – a grown-up wouldn't even have been able to reach its knee.

**Triceratops** was nine metres long and as big as an African elephant.

**Triceratops'** skull alone was three metres long.

**Stegosaurus** had a body as big as a bus, but a brain the size of a walnut.

The huge meat-eater **Spinosaurus** had a strange-looking sail of skin jutting up from its back, held up by spines, which were taller than a **fully grown human**.

In the past 40 years, fossils of larger and larger sauropods have been found – some more than 30 metres long. They have been given names like **Supersaurus**, **Ultrasaurus**, **Seismosaurus** and **Argentinosaurus**.

# BLOODTHIRSTY
## BEASTS

When **Tyrannosaurus rex** opened its jaws, its whole mouth could stretch sideways – all the better for gobbling up its victims.

**Tyrannosaurus rex** attacked by making a sudden dash towards its prey, then killing it with a savage bite to the neck.

Bloodthirsty **raptors** had huge curved pointed claws on their feet and hands – they attacked by **running** and **jumping** onto other animals and **slashing** with their claws.

**Utahraptor** was the biggest and **deadliest** raptor of all. With claws as long as a knife, it could cut a slice the length of a piano in its prey's flesh with one slash.

**Velociraptors** were smaller than Utahraptors, but just as deadly. They had sharp claws and could run up to 40 miles per hour.

**Velociraptor** ate **Protoceratops** – they have been found fossilised together in a battle to the death.

**Dromaeosaurus** had powerful jaws lined with teeth that looked like saws.

**Stegosaur** had a dangerous tail, with spikes on the end, and **powerful muscles** – perfect for inflicting a serious wound.

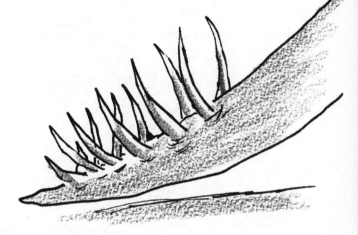

If **Plateosaurus** reared up on its hind legs, it could have used the claws on its front feet (normally used for raking leaves together) as a **weapon** against attackers.

Speed was important for a smaller hunter, like **Velociraptor**, who made high-speed chases after its victims before seizing them in its sharp claws.

Some raptors hunted in packs just like hunting dogs do today.

Huge plant-eaters like **Apatosaurus** used their claws for important things like gathering food, but they could also be vicious weapons.

As well as using their size and weight as weapons against meat-eaters, the giant plant-eaters could also **lash their tails** from side to side to defend themselves.

# AMAZING
# ARMOUR

The **anklylosaurs**, **stegosaurs** and **ceratopsians** may have looked terrifying but they were plodding plant-eaters and needed their amazing armour to protect themselves from meat-eating predators.

**Stegosaurus** was protected from predators like **Allosaurus** by the big bony plates standing up on its back.

The bone-headed dinosaur, **Stygimoloch**, had a thick skull to head-butt attackers like **Dromaeosaurus**, and its whole head was covered in small horns and bumps.

Plant-eating boneheads like **Pachycephalosaurus** and **Stegoceras** had dome-shaped skulls that were **40 times thicker** than a human skull. Some scientists believe that boneheads took part in head-butting battles to decide who should be the leader of the pack.

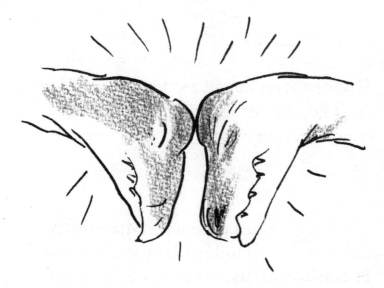

**Ankylosaurus** had a massive lump of bone on the end of its tail, which was powerful enough to break the bones of a **Tyrannosaurus rex**.

When **Stegosaurus** got angry, scientists think it pumped **blood** into its plates to make them turn red and look even scarier.

**Triceratops** frightened enemies away with its head of horns and spikes. Its horns were almost as tall as a fully grown human being!

**Styracosaurus** had a large spiny frill, with six long spines that pointed back over its neck, making it look larger and scarier.

Grown-up ceratopsian dinosaurs like **Protoceratops** protected their babies by standing in a circle around them and shaking their horned heads to scare away predators.

**Pentaceratops** had the most horns – five all together – one on its nose, one above each eye and one on each cheek.

The ankylosaur dinosaurs, **Ankylosaurus**, **Acanthopholis**, **Silvisaurus** and **Nodosaurus**, defended themselves from attackers like **Tyrannosaurus rex** with the heavy armour of plates all over their bodies.

**Ankylosaurs** had a second layer of bones over its normal skull bones. Even its **eyelids** were made of bone! Weird!

The only way a ferocious flesh-eater could attack **Ankylosaurus** was to flip it over and attack its unprotected part – its soft tummy.

# BONES AND BODY BITS

Most dinosaurs had about **350 bones** in their skulls and skeletons. That's **144 more** than an adult human skeleton.

Ankylosaur dinosaurs had the most bones because of all their armour – **300 bony plates** and spines along its back, as well as 50 extra plates around its head and **hundreds** of small bone plates in the skin.

**Brachiosaurus'** long neck contained 15 bones – more than giraffes, who only have seven.

The thigh bone of a **Compsognathus** was only 11 cm long, about the same length as an ice lolly stick.

Did you know that stegosaur's plates had blood vessels in them? These may have soaked up the **heat from the sun** and kept them warm.

**Saurolophus** had a long bony spike on its forehead, which it used to make calling sounds, and **Parasaurolophus** had a long hollow crown attached to its nose that it used to make loud honking noises.

Hadrosaur dinosaurs like **Corythosaurus** had crests on top of their heads, in all shapes and sizes. Scientists think these crests helped them to recognise each other.

The duck-billed dinosaur **Edmontosaurus** didn't have a crest, but scientists think it had an area of loose skin on top of its snout which blew up like a balloon to make a bellowing call.

# MONSTERS
# ON THE
# MOVE

Before the dinosaurs, reptiles moved with their legs sticking out sideways, like **lizards** do today, but dinosaurs' legs were straight down underneath their bodies, so they could carry more weight.

Scientists can tell how fast dinosaurs moved by looking at the distance between their **fossilised footprints** and comparing them to the leg length of the dinosaur.

Fossilised tracks also reveal which species of dinosaurs travelled together in herds.

Weighed down by their **heavy armour**, stegosaurs moved slowly. They could trot along at around ten miles an hour – Aerobic Al could easily have beaten one in a race!

**Lazy Linda . . . hmm, maybe not.**

Plant-eating anklyosaurs, like **Acanthopholis**, were even slower. Their maximum speed was six miles an hour, about the **jogging speed** of a human.

**Tyrannosaurus rex** was too heavy to go very fast. Instead of running after its prey, it would hide, then suddenly charge out with its **huge jaws** wide open. **Aaaagh!**

But **Tyrannosaurus rex** had to be careful when it was charging. If it tripped, its arms were too short and weak to break its fall.

If the giant plant-eaters had tried to run, scientists think they would have broken their legs, because their leg bones wouldn't have been able to withstand the impact.

Bonehead dinosaurs like **Stegoceras** needed their straight, stiff tails to balance out the weight of their heavy heads when they were running. Without them, they would have overbalanced!

**Velociraptors** could run at 40 miles per hour for short bursts – that's as fast as a racehorse, and definitely faster than Aerobic Al!

# TERRIBLE
# TEETH

Teeth fossils are a great way for scientists to work out what dinosaurs ate. They compare fossils with the teeth of animals that are around today.

If a dinosaur was a meat-eater, it would have had **sharp, pointed teeth**. Plant-eaters' teeth were usually rounded and more blunt.

**Tyrannosaurus rex's** teeth were as big as bananas. They were shaped like **knives**, but a lot sharper – perfect for tearing the flesh off its victims and crushing their bones!

**Allosaurus** had sharp, saw-edged teeth for slicing through meat. They curved backwards to give Allosaurus a firm grip on its victims.

**Oviraptor** had a sharp beak instead of teeth. Scientists don't know for sure what they ate, but the heads of little **Troodon** dinosaurs have been found in an oviraptor's nest, so they may have eaten meat.

**Diplodocus** had long, thin teeth, shaped like pencils – perfect for snipping at plants.

**Stegosaurs** had teeth with a frilly edge for cutting through leaves. But these weren't very powerful, so stegosaurs could only eat soft leaves and plants.

**Edmontosaurus** chopped leaves with the toothless beak at the front of its jaws. Further back, rows of tiny tightly-packed teeth formed a grinding surface to break the food down.

Scientists can estimate the height of plant-eating dinosaurs by looking at their teeth because they show the **sorts of food** the dinosaur would have eaten.

**Brachiosaurus** had long, thin teeth at the front of its jaws. With its long neck, it could stretch up to the fresh tender leaves at the very tops of trees.

Larger horned dinosaurs, like **Triceratops**, had short necks. They used their sharp beaks to bite off mouthfuls of plants.

The smallest plant-eaters, like **Protoceratops**, would have had strong teeth to chop up the tough plants on the ground.

# GREEDY GUTS

Palaeontologists study fossils of dinosaur dung to find out what dinosaurs ate. **Blecccch!**

**Tyrannosaurus rex** produced **giant poo** – a sample was discovered that was one metre long. Yeuch!

**Tyrannosaurus rex** could eat as much as 230 kilograms of meat and bones – that's about the weight of a whole calf – in just one mouthful!

Tyrannosaurs had such short arms that they weren't even long enough to push food into their mouths. But T-rex had an **excellent sense of smell** – perfect for sniffing out its next victim!

Palaeontologists have found **bite marks** on the bones of two tyrannosaurs — they think the dinosaurs fought to the **death**, and then the winner ate the loser. Scary!

Scientists have even found a dinosaur's last meal fossilised in its stomach.

**Allosaurus** probably took a few big bites of its victim, then left it alone while it grew too weak to fight back, before returning for the kill.

Most giant plant-eaters, like **Apatosaurus**, probably munched non-stop, like cows do today, because they needed to eat a lot of food before they were full. A bit like Greedy Graham!

**Diplodocus** needed to eat about five tonnes of plants every day – that's a pile as big as a house.

**Stegosaurs'** front legs were half the size of their back legs so that their heads tilted down and they could easily feed near the ground.

Some of the plant-eating dinosaurs' teeth
weren't strong enough to chew up tough
leaves, so they also swallowed small rocks to
help break down their food.

**Plateosaurus** had strong hands and a broad,
muscular thumb with a deep claw on it,
which it used to rake leaves together and push
them into its mouth.

Ankylosaur dinosaurs like **Nodosaurus** and **Ankylosaurus** had to eat the lower plants because they couldn't reach higher than a door handle.

# NEW NAMES

If you **discover a dinosaur**, you're allowed to **choose its name**.

Dinosaurs' names are chosen to describe something unusual about their bodies, or after the place where their fossils were found, or the person who found them.

**Compsognathus** means 'pretty jaw'

**Stegosaurus** means 'roofed reptile'

**Spinosaurus** means 'spiny lizard'

**Pentaceratops** means 'five-horned head'

**Triceratops** means 'three-horned face'

**Deinonychus** means 'terrible claw'

**Velociraptor** means 'speedy thief'

**Corythosaurus** means 'helmet lizard'

**Troodon** means 'wounding tooth'

**Megalosaurus** means 'great lizard'

**Saltopus** means 'leaping foot'

**Tyrannosaurus rex** means 'tyrant lizard king'

**Utahraptor** was discovered in Utah in the USA.

**Argentinosaurus** was found in Argentina in South America.

**Wuerhosaurus** was discovered in Wuerho in China.

A married pair of palaeontologists named dinosaurs after their two children – **Leaellynasaura** after their daughter Leaellyn and **Timimus** after her little brother Tim.

The name **Dracorex Hogwartsia**, meaning
'Dragon King of Hogwarts' – was given to
a dinosaur who looked like the sort of
fantastical dragon encountered by Harry Potter.

The biggest, best-preserved **Tyrannosaurus
rex** skeleton has been nicknamed 'Sue' after
the woman who discovered her.

# EXTRAORDINARY
# EGGS

Palaeontologists have found fossilised eggs and remains of nests, so they know that, **just like birds**, baby dinosaurs grew inside eggs laid by their mothers.

Most dinosaurs built nests of soil and leaves to keep their eggs safe and warm until they were ready to hatch.

Most dinosaurs were **too big** to sit on their eggs without crushing them.

Some lighter-weight dinosaurs, like **Troodon** and **Oviraptor**, sat on their eggs until they hatched.

Oviraptor was good at caring for its young, but its name means **'egg thief'**. Scientists first believed that the reason it was found near nest fossils was because it stole other dinosaurs' eggs. They later discovered that the eggs actually belonged to Oviraptor.

Dinosaur eggshells were often ten times thicker than a hen's eggshell.

Brachiosaurus' eggs were as **big as footballs**!

Brachiosaurus eggs have been discovered in a line and not in a nest, so scientists believe that the eggs were laid while Brachiosaurus was walking.

Baby dinosaurs had a special **sharp tooth**, which they used to chip their way out of their eggs.

The duck-billed dinosaur's eggs were about 18 cm long – roughly three times the size of a chicken's egg.

Even the most enormous dinosaurs had small babies – in fact, some grown-up dinosaurs were **200 times bigger** than their babies!

# BIGGEST, SMALLEST, FIERCEST, TALLEST...

**First-ever dinosaurs** – Herrerasaurus and Eoraptor, fast-running meat-eaters that lived about 230 million years ago.

**First dinosaur to be named** – Megalosaurus, meaning 'great lizard', was named in 1824.

**Biggest** – Argentinosaurus, at 35 metres long – the length of three buses – is the largest land animal ever found.

**Smallest** – Microraptor was only about 40 cm long -- the size of a crow.

**Heaviest** – Brachiosaurus at 80 tonnes. That's the same as 17 elephants. Phew!

**Tallest** – Sauroposeidon, at 18.5 metres tall, like three giraffes standing on top of each other.

**Fiercest** – Utahraptor, even though it didn't look as ferocious as Tyrannosaurus rex, it moved more quickly and hunted in a pack which made it extra-scary and dangerous.

**Biggest meat-eater** – Giganotosaurus, a huge hunter over 12 metres long, even bigger than Tyrannosaurus rex and Utahraptor.

**Longest name** – Micropachycephalosaurus, meaning tiny thick-headed lizard. At 50 cm long, it was almost as small as the Microraptor.

**Shortest name** – Minmi, a small plant-eating dinosaur with bony plates on its body.

**Brainiest** – Troodon, a fast-moving meat-eating dinosaur. It had the biggest brain compared to the size of its body and its large eyes were perfect for hunting at night.

**Stupidest** – Apatosaurus had the smallest brain compared to the size of its body – which was about 100,000 times bigger than its brain!

**So Beefy Bert is smarter, but not by much. Tee hee.**

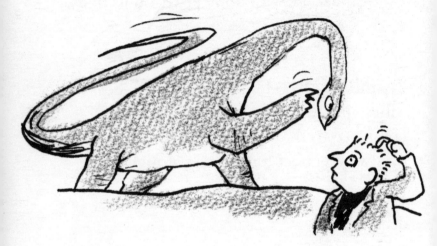

**Oldest** – Scientists think Apatosaurus and Brachiosaurus lived to be 100 years old.

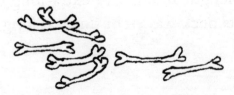

**Fastest** – Gallimimus, it could run at up to 43 miles per hour.

**Longest tail** – Diplodocus, its tail was about 13 metres long – the length of a double-decker bus.

**Longest neck** – Mamenchisaurus, its 15-metre-long neck made up about half of its total length and had 19 extra-long neck bones. Its neck was eight times as long as a giraffe's!

**Biggest head** – Triceratops had the biggest skull of any land animal that has ever lived. At almost three metres long, it was half the length of its whole body.

**Longest claws** – the plant-eating Therizinosaurus's claws measured an amazing 70 cm! Very handy for defending itself against meat-eaters.

# STRANGE
# BUT TRUE...

Scientists can tell from fossils they've found that some of today's animals, like **crocodiles** and **sharks**, were around at the same time as the dinosaurs.

Dinosaurs would have been able to walk from Africa to America because all the land was joined together.

**Birds** are descended from dinosaurs. Scientists believe this because some dinosaurs, like **Velociraptor**, have bones similar to a large bird. Both birds and dinosaurs lay eggs, and some dinosaur fossils have been found with feathers.

Dinosaurs' skins were probably much like that of a crocodile today, with a leathery surface and protective bony lumps.

The huge **Apatosaurus** could swim – but it put a foot on the mud at the bottom every now and then. What a cheat!

Scientists compared the size of dinosaurs' brain cavities to the size of their body and concluded that meat-eaters were **much cleverer** than the giant plant-eaters.

**Coprolite** is the scientific name for dinosaur poo!

The people of Ancient China thought dinosaur fossils were the **teeth of dragons** and ground them up to use in their medicines.

# MYTHBUSTERS

Most of the dinosaurs were **not** fierce flesh-eaters. Only one dinosaur in 20 actually ate meat. The rest were **harmless vegetarians**, who would have enjoyed dining at The Virtuous Veggie.

Not all of the fearsome flesh-eaters were huge – **Compsognathus** was the size of a **chicken**. It hunted insects and other tiny creatures.

Some huge prehistoric animals weren't dinosaurs at all. The sail-backed **Dimetrodon** was a mammal, and more closely related to human beings than to dinosaurs.

There were **never any human beings** around during the age of the dinosaurs – not even cavemen!

There wasn't really a dinosaur that **sprayed poison** into a predator's eyes. **Dilophosaurus** did this in the film **Jurassic Park**, but there's no evidence that it's actually true.

There **weren't any** flying or swimming dinosaurs. **Pterodactyl** was a flying reptile, and **Plesiosaurus** was a marine reptile, but they couldn't be classified as dinosaurs because they didn't stand upright.

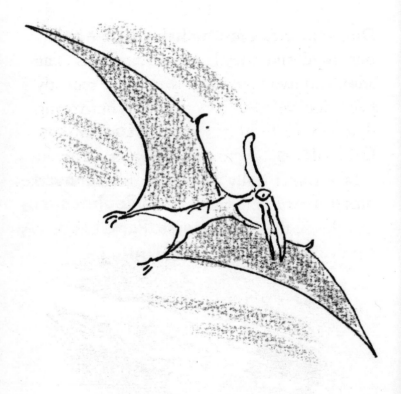

**Diplodocus** and **Apatosaurus** didn't eat leaves from high up in the trees. Even though they had very long necks, they couldn't lift their heads much more than **five metres** off the ground.

Dinosaurs didn't just walk the Earth – they burrowed underneath it too. The fossils of an adult and two young dinosaurs have recently been discovered in a burrow. This burrowing dinosaur has been named **Oryctodromeus Cubicularis**: orycto means 'digger', dromeus means 'runner' and 'cubicularis' means that the dinosaur built a den.

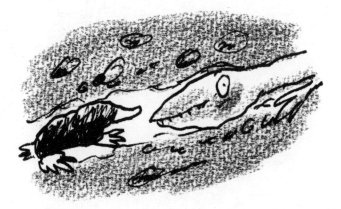

There's no such dinosaur as **Brontosaurus**! A palaeontologist thought he'd discovered two different dinosaurs – **Apatosaurus** and **Brontosaurus** – but later he realised that all the bones were actually from the same dinosaur, so it had to be called by the first name he'd chosen – Apatosaurus.

# DEATH OF THE DINOSAURS

Dinosaurs died out **65 million years ago**.

**But why?** Did they go **slowly** or **quickly**? What *really* happened? Scientists have lots of **different** ideas.

Was it a **long, drawn out death** as volcanoes violently erupted for a million years and poisoned the air?

Did an **asteroid** and the **volcanoes** change the weather, so that it grew colder and the seas began to dry up?

Did the dinosaurs' favourite kinds of plants die out, so that the plant-eaters couldn't find food?

And, without the plant-eaters to prey on, did the meat-eaters eventually **starve to death** too?

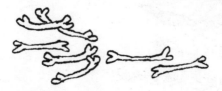

Or was it a sudden death when a **huge asteroid** from **outer space** hit the Earth, sending tonnes of boiling rock and gas into the air and enormous waves crashing over the land?

Or was it a **mixture** of all these ideas?

Scientists are still trying to find out **the truth** . . .

**Bye!**